DATE DUE

#1326

AG 3'90 JA 20 '03		
AG 17'91 JE 19 06		
NO 5'91 DE 06 13		
AG 13'92 MY 14 B		
AP 17'93 R 2 0 0		
MY 11'93 JE 2 2 78		
MR 25 '99		
JE 08 '00		
JY 26 01		
JF 25 01		
JY 25 02		
AG 15 '02		

J
636.5   Coldrey, Jennifer
COL   The world of chickens

Where Animals Live

The World of Chickens

Text by Jennifer Coldrey

Photographs by
Oxford Scientific Films

Gareth Stevens Publishing
Milwaukee

Where Chickens Live

Chickens are *domestic* birds. They are found mainly on farms. There, people can look after them. Not long ago, chickens were free to roam around the farmyard. They picked up food wherever they could find it.

On small farms, chickens are still kept this way. There are lots of places to explore in the farmyard.

On this farm, chickens can wander in a grassy field during the day. At night, they sleep in a chicken coop. There they are protected from foxes and other *predators*. Chickens which live outside this way are called "free-range." They are fed by the farmer. But they can also look for their own food.

A farm is not really a natural *habitat*. On it, animals are raised and taken care of by humans. On big, modern chicken farms, thousands of chickens are kept in large sheds.

3

Different Kinds of Chicken

All breeds of chicken come from the same ancestor — the wild Red Jungle Fowl. This chicken was tamed over 4,000 years ago by people in India and Southeast Asia. Then people began to breed it. Wild jungle fowl still live in Southeast Asian forests today. The Red Jungle Fowl above is a rooster.

Today there are over a hundred breeds of chicken. Some, like this White Leghorn, are small. They are mostly good for laying eggs. One chicken can lay 300 white eggs a year.

Some breeds are good for both laying eggs and eating. *Hybrids* are produced by mating different breeds. These often show the best qualities of both breeds.

Some smaller breeds, called *bantams,* can only lay small eggs. Bantams are kept on small farms for show.

This Rhode Island Red is a popular breed. One popular hybrid is a White Leghorn hen crossed with a Rhode Island Red rooster. The hen of this breed is a good egg-layer.

The Chicken's Body

Chickens come in many sizes, shapes, and colors. Their colors depend on the breed. Some are white. Others are black or brown. Sometimes the feathers are speckled. Or they are striped with different colors. The strong legs are covered with scales. The feet are good for walking and gripping. Roosters have an extra spike or spur sticking out from the leg (see picture above).

Chickens have plump bodies. They look even plumper because of their soft, silky feathers. Also, their tail feathers stick out. Chickens *molt,* or shed and replace, their feathers once a year.

 Chickens have small heads with sharp beaks. The flaps of loose skin hanging down from the throat are called *wattles*. On top of the head is a pink crest. This is called a *comb*. Roosters are larger and more colorful than hens. They also have larger combs and wattles.

Chickens are short, stout birds. Because their wings are short and weak, chickens do not fly very far.

Food and Feeding

Free-range chickens find plenty to eat around the farmyard. They use their feet and claws to find food in the ground. They use their sharp beaks for pecking at seeds and plants. They also eat insects and worms. They help the farmer by clearing away weeds and pests.

Usually the farmer will also feed free-range chickens wheat or corn. Farmers also use chicken feed from the store. Chickens will also eat scraps from the farmhouse.

Chickens must eat lots of green vegetables. Green food has vitamins and minerals. It also contains *pigments.* They make egg yolks a bright yellow.

Farmers must be sure chickens get enough calcium. Calcium helps make egg shells hard.

Chickens do not have teeth, so they must swallow food whole. They also swallow small stones. These are stored in a second stomach, or gizzard. There, the stones grind the food into small bits. Chickens also need plenty of fresh water to drink. ⬇

Habits and Behavior

Both domestic and wild chickens show many of the same habits. Wild jungle fowl *roost* at night in forest trees. There, they are safe from enemies on the forest floor. At night, farm chickens roost on special perches. Their toes lock onto the perch. Even if the chicken falls asleep, it won't fall off.

Like most birds, chickens *preen* their feathers. This helps get rid of fleas and other *parasites*.

Chickens also like to dust-bathe in dry, dusty dirt. The dust bath keeps chickens cool. It also helps get rid of parasites in the skin and feathers. Chickens never bathe in water.

Chickens are very noisy. They constantly cluck and squawk. This is how they communicate with each other. Of course, roosters have the loudest calls. Chickens also like to live in flocks. In any flock there is an order among the chickens. In this order, chickens range from the strongest and most bossy to the weakest and most timid. This order is called the "pecking order." Often the strong birds dominate the weaker ones, and fights may break out.

Courtship and Mating

Chickens mate all year round. The rooster mates with many different hens. He courts them by preening his feathers and strutting around. When mating, the rooster climbs on top of the hen. He then *fertilizes* the eggs that are inside the hen's body. Only fertilized eggs will hatch ⬇ into chicks.

On small farms there is usually only one *cockerel,* or young rooster, living with the hens. Roosters can be very jealous. Often they will fight over the hens. These two roosters are fighting. You can see how they fight with their feet and claws. They use their spurs to kick and tear at one another.

This rooster seems content enough. He is resting quietly with the hens in the farmyard.

Laying Eggs

Hens lay eggs most of their lives. It doesn't matter whether or not the eggs have been fertilized. Hens usually lay one egg a day.

Wild chickens would lay a *clutch* of eggs and wait for them to hatch. On the modern farm, however, the eggs are taken away every day. This keeps the chickens laying. This is how farm chickens can lay 300 a year. Wild chickens only lay about 50 eggs a year.

Hens need warm nests to lay their eggs in. On the farm, hens sometimes find unusual places on their own.

Most chickens on modern farms are given nesting boxes. These boxes are in the chicken coop.

Eggs are first made in the hen's *ovary*. One egg cell is made each day. The egg passes down through the chicken's body. As it does, the white and shell form around the yolk. When the egg is first laid, the shell is moist. It quickly dries and hardens.

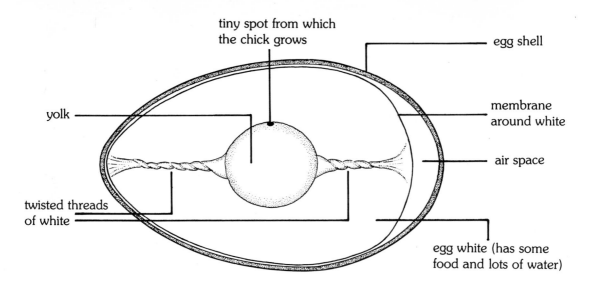

tiny spot from which the chick grows

egg shell

yolk

membrane around white

air space

twisted threads of white

egg white (has some food and lots of water)

Growth Inside the Fertile Egg

A chicken's egg gives all the food a growing chick will need. It is rich in food for people, too. Most of the goodness comes from the yolk. The white gives some food and lots of water. The shell has hundreds of tiny holes to let air in so the *embryo* can breathe. The egg also has an air space. As the chick grows, it will need this for breathing.

At first, the baby chick is a spot only 1/25 inch long. But the embryo grows fast. After 10 weeks (above), it is 1½ inches long. The head, wings, and legs are formed, and feathers have started to grow. As the chick grows, blood vessels spread over the yolk. These bring food and oxygen to the embryo.

Young chicks will grow only if the eggs are kept warm, or *incubated*. The natural way is for a *broody* hen to sit on them. She will turn the eggs two or three times a day. This warms them evenly. She will sit on a clutch of eggs for three weeks. This is how long they take to hatch.

On modern farms, fertile eggs are kept in heated boxes. These are called incubators. Machines turn the eggs and control the temperature.

17

Hatching into Young Chicks

A few days before the eggs are hatched,
the chicks begin cheeping inside their
shells. The baby chick chips at the shell
from inside. First the chick makes a rough
line around the middle of the shell. It
then breaks the shell apart. It can take 14
hours for a chick to hatch.

The eggs in one clutch are laid a few days
apart. But the chicks only start to grow
when the whole clutch is laid. That is why
all the eggs hatch within a few hours of
each other.

The chick is wet and tired when it first hatches. Soon it dries into a fluffy ball of down.

Chicks stay close together. They also continually cheep. This lets the mother know where they are. She keeps them warm at night. On farms with no broody hen, young chicks stay warm under electric heaters.

At first, chicks live on the yolk remains in their bodies. After a day or two, they learn to peck for their own food.

Growing Up

After two or three weeks, the chicks start
to lose their down and grow real feathers.
As they get older, it is easy to tell the
males from the females. The comb on the
young rooster, or cockerel, starts to grow
at four or five weeks. This is earlier than
on a young hen, which is called a *pullet*.
After six weeks, the chicks are well-grown.
By nine weeks, they have moved into
some kind of poultry house. These young
chickens (above) are ten weeks old. They
have learned to perch.

Cockerels are kept for breeding or providing meat. Farmers keep pullets mainly for egg-laying. Pullets start laying eggs when they are just five months old. They cannot lay fertile eggs until they are a year old. On big farms, laying hens are kept for 18 months. Then they are killed for meat. When chickens are raised only for eating, males and females are fattened quickly. They are killed at about nine weeks. If laying chickens are not killed, they can live up to 12 years.

These pullets are just five months old. They have started to lay eggs. ➡

Enemies and Other Dangers

Chickens are cared for by people. They still have enemies, however. The fox is one of the chicken's worst enemies. At night, foxes come into farmyards to look for chickens. To keep foxes out, chicken coops must be locked up tight.

Other animals attack chickens, too. These include badgers, mink, weasels, and stoats. Rats (right) steal chicken feed, kill young chicks, and eat eggs. Even cats and dogs may chase and catch young chicks.

Chickens have few defenses against their enemies. They are nervous birds, and they panic easily.

Chickens have smaller enemies, too. Many parasites infect chickens on their bodies. Parasites can spread diseases and cause death in young chicks. Sometimes chickens have to be sprayed with *insecticides* to get rid of parasites. Chickens can also catch colds and other diseases that spread through a coop.

Chickens and Humans

Chickens have been raised by humans for thousands of years. Some ancient peoples used them for religious sacrifices. Others used them to fight for sport. This rooster (below) has a huge crest of feathers on his head. This Chinese Silkie bantam (right) has soft, fluffy feathers. Both birds have been bred as show birds.

The ancient Chinese kept domestic hens. So did the ancient Egyptians, Greeks, and Romans. By the year 100, chickens had been brought to Western Europe. The Spanish introduced them to the Americas in the 1500s.

This picture is from 18th century Persia (Iran). It shows cockfighting. Cockfighting was first popular in Asia and then Europe and the Americas. Around the middle of the 19th century, many countries put a stop to cockfighting.

Chickens have always been used as food by humans. But people only started to breed chickens for eating about a hundred years ago. Some birds are bred for eating only. Some are bred for egg-laying only. Some are bred for both. It is not only farmers who raise chickens. Some people keep chickens for pets.

Life on a Modern Poultry Farm

At one time, most farm chickens were free-range. They would be let outside during the daytime. At night, they would be kept in a coop. Today, however, there is more demand for chicken eggs and meat. Most chickens are now kept on huge, modern poultry farms. Thousands of birds are raised in large buildings (above). There are special farms for every use of a chicken you can imagine.

Egg-laying hens are kept on egg-laying farms. Here, chickens live in wire cages with three to five birds in one cage. As the eggs are laid, they roll down into a trough. This trough collects the eggs. The hens eat and drink from a large trough in front of the cages.

Another special farm is a *broiler* farm. Broilers are chickens that are raised for their meat. A broiler house is a large shed with no windows. There are perches for the chickens to roost on. As many as 20,000 chickens may be kept in one shed.

Chickens lay more eggs in the light than in the dark. That is why egg-laying farms keep the light on for many hours. Most egg-laying farms are warm and clean and safe from enemies. In the summer, they may even let in fresh air and sunshine (below). Still, some people would rather pay more money at the store for chickens raised free-range. They feel it is less cruel. And they feel their meat and eggs taste better, too.

Friends and Neighbors

Chickens on a modern poultry farm see only one other kind of animal: the people who take care of them. On an older style of farm, there are many other kinds of animals around. In this picture, a White Silkie hen and her chicks share their food with ducks and geese.

Ducks and geese may desert their eggs. Sometimes a farmer will use a broody hen to hatch and raise baby ducks and geese. After hatching, the ducklings and goslings will treat the hen as their own mother.

Most farms have dogs and cats, too. ⬆
Cats do not bother chickens too much, and
they help keep away mice and rats. Wild
birds will often eat chicken feed. They do
not eat enough to matter to the chickens.
But they do bring in diseases. These
diseases may be picked up by the chickens.

On some free-range farms, the chickens
are allowed to roam the fields. You can
sometimes see cows and chickens in the
same pastures. ⬇

Life on the Farm

On a free-range farm chickens depend on their habitat for food. Their diet is made up of plants, small animals, and some grain from the farmer. This food is passed on to predators that eat the chickens. This forms a food chain.

On modern farms, the diet is more controlled. But it is still made up mostly of natural plants and animals. People are the main consumers of chickens. This chart shows us how the chicken's diet is linked to our own.

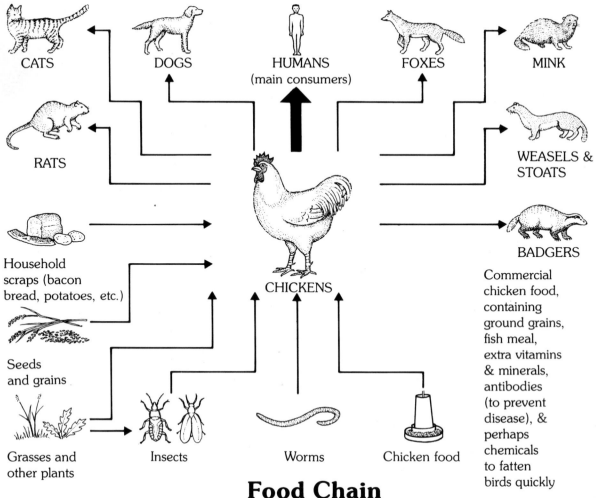

CATS

DOGS

HUMANS
(main consumers)

FOXES

MINK

RATS

WEASELS &
STOATS

Household
scraps (bacon
bread, potatoes, etc.)

CHICKENS

BADGERS

Seeds
and grains

Commercial
chicken food,
containing
ground grains,
fish meal,
extra vitamins
& minerals,
antibodies
(to prevent
disease), &
perhaps
chemicals
to fatten
birds quickly

Grasses and
other plants

Insects

Worms

Chicken food

Food Chain

Chickens on an older style of farm ⬆
usually have a healthy and contented life.
They are given food and shelter by the
farmer. And they are free to scratch around
in the open for their own natural foods.

Life may not seem so good on a modern
poultry farm. Chickens live in crowded
rooms or cages, and they don't get any
fresh air or sunshine. At least they are
warm and safe from predators.

Chickens on any type of farm usually are
killed for food. During their short lives, it
is important that we care for them well, as
we would any animal.

New Words About Chickens

These new words about chickens appear in the text in *italics*, just as they appear here.

bantam........... a very small breed of chicken
broiler........... a chicken raised for its meat
broody .... the mothering instinct of a hen; it makes her want to sit on eggs and raise chicks
clutch .... a set of eggs
cockerel .... a male chicken under one year old
comb .... the fleshy part on top of a chicken's head
domestic........ tamed and kept by humans
embryo......... the very early stages of an animal's growth, before it is born or hatched
fertilize .... to join a male sperm cell with a female's egg, so that a new individual can grow from the fertilized egg
habitat .... the place where an animal or plant lives
hybrid........... an animal or plant produced by crossing or mating two different breeds or kinds
incubated....... (of eggs) kept warm so that they will hatch
insecticides...... chemicals used to kill insect pests
molt .... to shed feathers and replace them with new ones
ovary .... a female sex organ which produces eggs
parasites........ animals (or plants) that live and feed on others
pigments........ colored substances found in animals and plants
predators .... animals that kill and eat other animals
preen .... to clean the feathers by stroking and combing them with the bill
pullet........... a female chicken under one year old
roost .... to sleep or rest
wattles .... loose flaps of skin hanging down from either side of a chicken's face

Reading level analysis: SPACHE 2.4, FRY 2, FLESCH 92 (very easy),
RAYGOR 3, FOG 3, SMOG 3

Library of Congress Cataloging-in-Publication Data

Coldrey, Jennifer.
  The world of chickens.

  (Where animals live)
  Summary: Simple text and photographs depict chickens feeding, breeding, and defending themselves in their natural habitats.
  [1. Chickens — Juvenile literature. [1. Chickens] I. Oxford Scientific Films. II. Title. III. Series.
SF487.5.C65   1986   636.5   86-5718

ISBN 1-55532-096-1
ISBN 1-55532-071-6 (lib. bdg.)

North American edition first published in 1987 by

Gareth Stevens, Inc.
7221 West Green Tree Road   Milwaukee, WI 53223, USA

U.S. edition, this format, copyright © 1987 by Belitha Press Ltd.
Text copyright © 1987 by Gareth Stevens, Inc.
Photographs copyright © 1987 by Oxford Scientific Films.

All rights reserved. No part of this book may be reproduced in any form or by any means without permission in writing from Gareth Stevens, Inc.

First conceived, designed, and produced by Belitha Press Ltd., London, as *The Chicken on the Farm*, with an original text copyright by Oxford Scientific Films. Format copyright by Belitha Press Ltd.

Design: Naomi Gaines.   Typeset by Ries Graphics ltd., Milwaukee.
Cover Design: Gary Moseley.   Printed in Hong Kong by South China Printing Co.
Line Drawings: Lorna Turpin.   Series Editor: Mark J. Sachner.
Scientific Consultants: Gwynne Vevers & David Saintsing.   Art Director: Treld Bicknell.

Photography **Oxford Scientific Films Ltd.** for pp. 1, 2, 3, 5 *both*, 7 *above*, 8, 9, 10 *both*, 11, 12 *below*, 13, 14, 15 *both*, 16, 20, 29 *below*, 31 and front cover (photographer G. I. Bernard); p. 4 (photographer David Cayless); pp. 6, 12 *above*, and 19 *above* (photographer David Thompson); pp. 7 *below*, 24 *below*, and 25 (photographers P. and W. Ward); pp. 17, 23 (photographer Peter Parks); p. 18 (photographer J. A. L. Cooke); p. 19 *below* (photographer Tony Allen); pp. 21, 26, 28, 29 *above*, and back cover (photographer Avril Ramage); p. 22 (photographer Robin Redfern); p. 27 (photographer Z. Leszczynsky); p. 24 *above* (cockfighting from an 18th century Persian text, courtesy of the British Museum).

32